THE 60s

Publishers: Telstar Records Ltd., The Studio,
5 King Edward Mews, Byfeld Gardens, Barnes,
London SW13 9HP.

This edition compiled in 1987 by Omnibus Press for
Telstar Books, a division of Telstar Records Limited.

© Copyright 1987 Omnibus Press
(A Division of Book Sales Limited)

ISBN 1 870759 04 4

Editor: Chris Charlesworth
Photo Research: Mary McCartney
Art Direction: Mike Bell
Book Design: Mainartery
Cover Design: The Snap Organisation
Typesetting: Capital Setters
Printing: St Ives Printing Group
Picture Credits: Rex Features, Topham Picture
Library.
Exclusive distributors:
Telstar Records Ltd.,
The Studio,
5 King Edward Mews,
Byfeld Gardens,
Barnes,
London SW13 9HP.

A new decade always brings new hope. Like moving house, changing jobs, saying goodbye to the last 10 years in the same breath as welcoming in the next holds with it the promise of rebirth; the King is dead, long live the King. It doesn't matter that history has shown us, again and again, that it simply doesn't work like that, that yesterday's problems have a nasty habit of turning up again tomorrow, the feeling is still there. And why not? There is, they say, an exception to every rule; the Sixties were that exception.

Even as the Fifties began sliding into oblivion, there was a sense of optimism hanging there. In Africa, the rising tide of nationalism had already seen Ghana win independence. Behind them, the queue for similar recognition was growing all the time. The Cold War, that drawn-out clash of the super powers, fought almost exclusively behind locked doors and with no weapon more deadly than microphones and earplugs, was finally thawing. The British Prime Minister, Harold MacMillan, had just returned from Moscow, while the Russian premier, Nikita Kruschev became the first Soviet head to visit the U.S. Further afield, the space race was on in earnest, the Russian Sputnik and American Explorer satellites having been placed into orbit within months of one another. As those first, hesitant steps were made it was hard to believe that within a decade man would walk first in space, and then on the surface of the moon itself... hard to believe, but not impossible.

By 1961, John F. Kennedy, America's 35th President and one whose election, the previous November, did as much to usher in the new optimism as any other single event, was already pledging his country to landing a man on the moon before the decade was over.

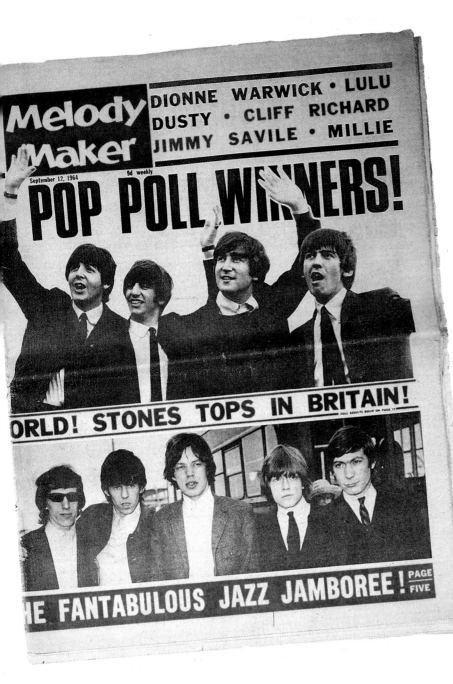

Melody Maker

September 12, 1964   9d weekly

DIONNE WARWICK • LULU
DUSTY • CLIFF RICHARD
JIMMY SAVILE • MILLIE

POP POLL WINNERS!

...ORLD! STONES TOPS IN BRITAIN!

FULL RESULTS BEGIN ON PAGE 17

...HE FANTABULOUS JAZZ JAMBOREE! PAGE FIVE

The Animals

The Move

Jim Morrison

Pop music was the soundtrack to all of this activity. First it was The Beatles, whose emergence in 1962 with 'Love Me Do' sparked a whole wave of pop talent which owed little to any recent trends in the music industry. Less than a year before, The Beatles had been turned down by a record company chief who told them, 'Sorry boys, but guitar groups are on the way out'. But no sooner had The Beatles chalked up their first chart-topper than every able-bodied guitar picker from Lands End to John O'Groats was queueing up for one or other of the contracts which were being handed around like candy.

Originally it was only Liverpool which mattered, but when that city had been cleaned out, the moguls had no alternative but to turn their attention to the other large, industrial cities. In Birmingham, Mike Sheridan's Nightriders took the first steps in a career which would eventually see them blossom into The Move and later, the Electric Light Orchestra. In Newcastle, the Alan Price Combo became The Animals; in London Manfred Mann, The Who and The Kinks all followed in footsteps first planted by The Beatles before heading off in their own separate directions.

Outside the cities, too, things were hotting up. The Rolling Stones crawled out of deepest suburbia and proceeded to shake society to its foundations. The Yardbirds followed, and over the course of their five-year career gave rock 'n' roll three of the most influential guitarists of any era; Eric Clapton, Jeff Beck and Jimmy Page, who at the end of the decade was to lead Led Zeppelin to the very pinnacle of rock superstardom. Everywhere you went, every turn you took, there would be another rough beat combo howling the blues and screaming the odds, and if the next decade was to see so much unharnessed energy, and so many disparate talents blend together into a cohesive whole, then it was as much the influence of the decade in which they lived as the genius of the musicians themselves which enabled it to happen. Swinging London swung only to pop music; later, in Vietnam, soldiers fought to the sounds of The Doors, The Jefferson Airplane, Jimi Hendrix and The Grateful Dead, music which was conceived in an atmosphere of rebellion in America, and which needed nothing more than a radio or cassette recorder to translate it to an even more violent medium on the other side of the world. Nobody was free from its imagery; the conspiracy of youth which let no cause go without at least one public demonstration was both conceived and executed to the strains of a thousand transistor radios, each one blaring out its own peculiar mixture of devil's beat and demon's consciousness. When Mick Jagger appeared in the film 'Performance' as a sexually abandoned, drug-taking weirdo, people didn't look upon him as an actor playing a role, they saw him as Mick Jagger being Mick Jagger, and it didn't matter how many other bastions of civilisation he was able to infiltrate, be it an editorial in *The Times* or a late night chat show for the BBC, he was still Lucifer incarnate and as responsible for the unrest which shook the western world at the end of the decade as any rubber-lipped, elastic-hipped pouting pop star ever could be.

Above: Two line-ups of the Yardbirds with Jeff Beck (above) and Eric Clapton (right) and Led Zeppelin (right) with Jimmy Page.

Mick Jagger

SIXTIES

On April 12 1961, Vostok 1 lifted off from the Baikonur Cosmodrome, making a single orbit of the earth before returning. The astronaut who accompanied it, Yuri Gagarin, became an instant hero, both at home and abroad. When he visited London later in the year, travelling in a Rolls Royce, YG1, thousands turned out to see him (tragically, Gagarin – like John Kennedy – was not to live to see the fulfilment of man's quest for the stars. He was killed in a flying accident in March, 1968, little more than a year before Apollo 11 deposited its human cargo on the lunar surface).

A second Vostok mission, in August 1961, piloted by cosmonaut Titov, was to make 17 orbits of the earth, and it wasn't until the following February that America put her first man into space, John Glenn. Thereafter, the Soviets were to have the edge on America almost until the last moment; in March 1965, Alexei Leonov became the first man to walk in space, the following February, Luna 9 became the first space craft to soft land on the moon itself; Luna 10 became the moon's first artificial satellite two months later.

The race into space, of course, was run, if not with mutual co-operation, at least with mutual respect, a spirit which culminated in the joint Russian-American ventures of the 1970s. Unfortunately, back on Mother Earth relations between the superpowers were not so cordial. The goodwill engendered by Nikita Kruschev's visit to President Eisenhower in 1959 was swiftly soured when it became evident that Russia had designs on the island of Cuba, where a revolutionary government headed by Fidel Castro supplanted the pro-American Batista regime, also in 1959. A counter-revolutionary force, financed by the U.S., was landed in the Bay Of Pigs, a last ditch bid to oust Castro's government, but within days it had been smashed, the weight of Castro's Soviet armaments taking even the Americans by surprise.

And it didn't matter where you went, still there was no escape from pop. When America launched the telecommunications satellite Telstar into space in 1962, the tiny box of tricks had barely started functioning before someone was at the top of the charts with a song about it. Seven years later, when Neil Armstrong and Buzz Aldrin took their giant step for mankind on the surface of the moon, there was David Bowie, still three years away from his own personal megastardom, relaying the sad story of Major Tom, an astronaut who liked it so much up there that he didn't ever want to come back down again.

Of course, while the West made all the headway in terms of putting Space in the charts, the East was putting it on the map.

Yuri Gagarin

From there the crisis lurched from bad to worse. Aerial photography revealed dark patches on the Cuban landscape which, expert analysis declared, marked projected Soviet missile bases. Immediately, the newly installed President Kennedy, calm even in the face of what was potentially the greatest threat ever to face an American President – that of all-out nuclear war – established a blockade of Cuban ports. Any vessel, Soviet or otherwise, which attempted breaking that blockade would be sunk. For a week in October 1962, the world shuddered on the brink of nuclear war, breathing again only when Kruschev yielded to Kennedy's demand; a complete withdrawal of Soviet forces from Cuba. The following year, three of the four nuclear powers – Russia, America and Great Britain, but not France – agreed a partial nuclear test ban; a year after that, 1964, Nikita Kruschev was removed from power in the U.S.S.R.

Soviet expansion did not, however, cease with the resolution of the Cuban missile crisis. Since the end of the World War Two, Berlin had been a divided city in name alone, with Checkpoint Charlie one of its busiest thoroughfares. In 1961, the traffic between the two sectors was effectively closed by the erection of the Berlin Wall. Smoke and mirrors were deployed to prevent Western television crews from filming the work in progress; East Germans making a last ditch bid for freedom did so at the risk of being shot and, as in case of teenager Peter Fechter, being left to die in the no-man's land which separated the two halves of the city.

Later, in August 1968, democratic reforms introduced by the Czechoslovak communists, headed by Alexander Dubček, were crushed even more harshly as Soviet tanks rolled into Prague whilst private Czech radio stations poured out a running commentary of events to a shocked, listening world. It was atrocities such as these, coupled with America's ever-burgeoning involvement in the Vietnamese conflict, and the battle for black civil rights in Uncle Sam's own backyard, which were to precipitate the upsurge of political consciousness enjoyed by western youth during the second half of the decade.

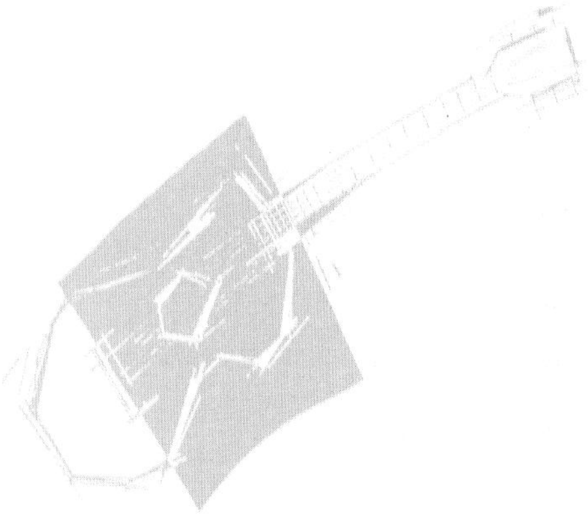

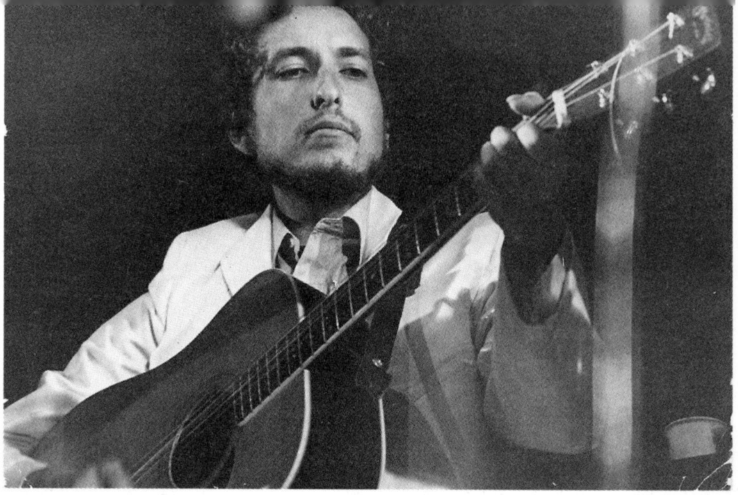

Bob Dylan

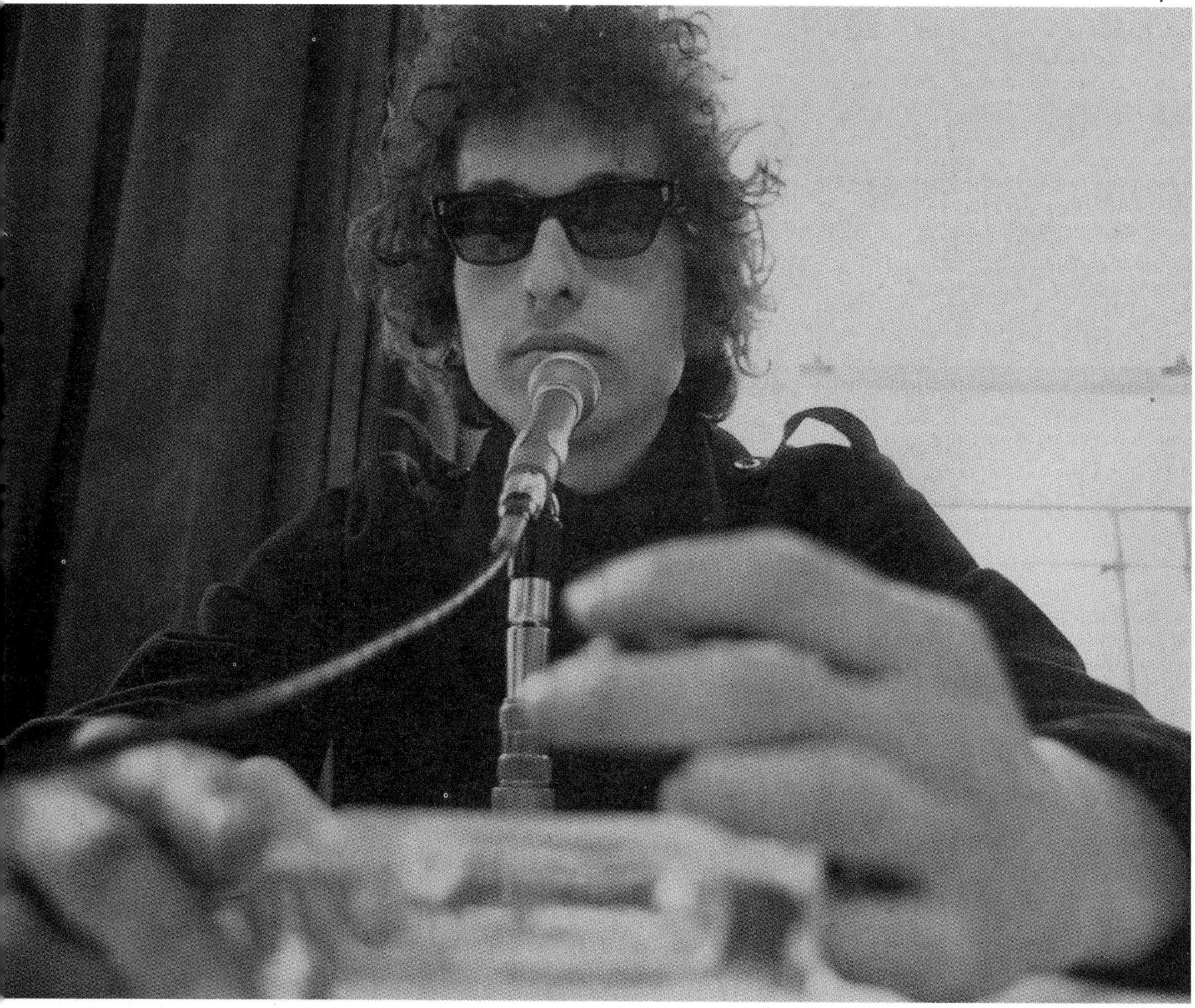

The spirit of rebellion which had been rock 'n' roll's calling card when it first burst forth in the mid-Fifties had long since been calmed; the Elvis Presley disgorged by the U.S. Army in 1960 was a totally different beast from the lip-sneering, hip-swinging demon who had *fallen-in* two years previously, other heroes were either dead, jailed or simply forgotten. And while the breakthrough of The Beatles, first in Britain but more importantly in America, did much to liberate pop from the strait-jacket of recent years, it was still to be several years before rock regained its roar. In its stead, the 'Protest' movement came screaming out of the American folk scene; Bob Dylan maintained a constant soundtrack to the Cuban crisis, then followed it up by accompanying the civil rights movement along its rocky road. With nothing more than a softly strummed guitar, an out-of-tune mouth harp and a nasal whine which could scarcely be described as a *singing* voice, he introduced a new literacy to youth culture. While The Beatles still sang 'Yeah Yeah Yeah', Dylan introduced us to the 'Masters Of War' and warned that a 'hard rain was gonna fall'. It didn't matter that it took the more wholesome charms of Peter Paul & Mary to bring his message to the widest possible audience, the points which Dylan hammered home eventually percolated to even the highest levels of society. And while it was not until he embraced rock, in 1965, that the music was able to come to terms with its own importance, but while the Vietnam war could have existed quite happily without rock 'n' roll, it is arguable that rock 'n' roll, or at least the culture which grew up around it, could ever have existed without Vietnam.

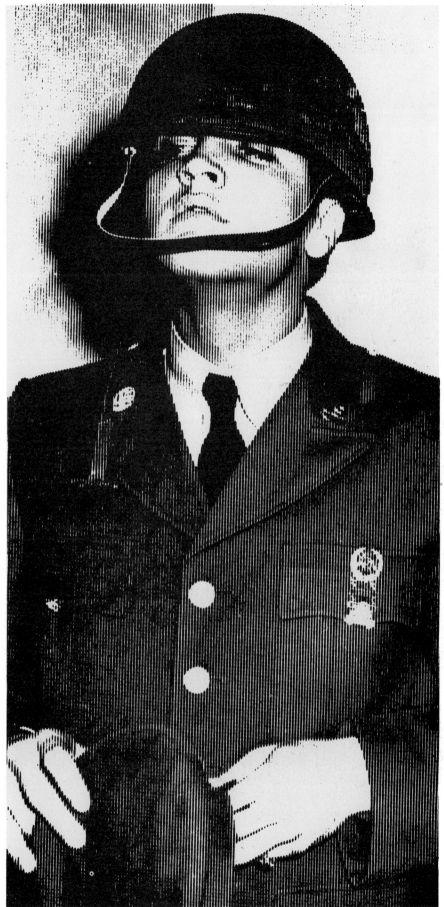

Elvis – GI 53310761 – Presley

The war had its roots in the French withdrawal from the former colony of Indo-China, following defeat at Dien Bien Phu in 1954. The victorious native forces immediately partitioned the territory, forming the independent states of Cambodia, Laos and Vietnam, with the latter being further divided into a democratic south and Communist north. Fearing a Communist take-over of the southern portion, America despatched first military advisers, then troops, in a bid to keep the peace. And on December 22, 1961, the first U.S. soldier, one of ten thousand troops in the country, was killed on active duty in Vietnam. Within seven years that total had risen to over half a million, and everybody knew somebody — or was somebody — whose right to life had been challenged by Mr. Draft-board. The protests began quietly, but so swiftly did the ceremonial draftcard burning catch on that no sooner had the media begun publicising it, than the government passed a bill outlawing it. Draft dodgers were either gaoled, or forced into exile — the boxer, Cassius Clay, was sentenced to five years imprisonment for refusing to fight for his country, the child specialist Dr. Spock received a similar sentence for assisting dodgers making their way out of the country. Against such a backdrop, an artform whose principal concern was to appeal to youth could not help but get serious. And while the number of acts who actually built their careers around the war was only a fraction of those who were to be considered 'anti-establishment', still it was the war which bound them together in the public estimation. And, of course, it was not long before the establishment itself cottoned on to the fact that, tragic though the war was, it was still binding together a vast number of people, and an equally vast number of potential record buyers. Suddenly the war, and the 60 thousand American servicemen who were to die throughout its course, became a commodity, as neatly packaged as love and cars and going to San Francisco with flowers in your hair.

John and Yoko in bed for peace.

The bands themselves were un-doubtedly sincere in their motives, but to the record companies who signed them they were simply fulfilling a demand. The kids want protests, we'll give them pro-tests. It was quite possibly the most callous marketing campaign ever launched, and so successful was it that most people weren't even aware of how many of the record companies involved in packaging the revolution were actually nothing more than subsidiaries of larger corporations who were equally bound up in the war itself. That, perhaps, was the ultimate irony; a war financed by the very people who protested against it.

The focal point for the revolution, of course, was America, or more precisely, California – the same California as had just voted a former movie actor, Ronald Reagan, into office as state governor. The streets of Haight-Ashbury, a downtrodden junction at the wrong end of San Francisco, spawned any number of hybrid talents, their music caught somewhere between a Bo Diddley beat and a post-hallucinogenic euphoria. But their music was irrelevant, simply a means of expression for a genera-tion who looked around at the world, and didn't like what they saw. When John and Yoko spent a week in bed, 'for peace', the straights thought it was just another publicity stunt and wondered how the pair would cope with the bedsores. Everybody else fell for it hook, line and sinker.

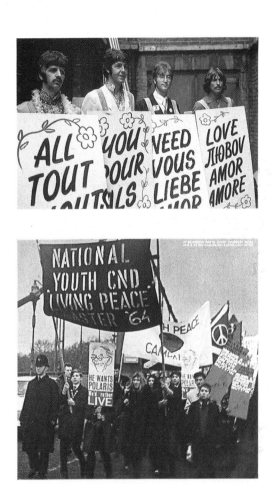

The Beatles (top) and John's psychedelic Rolls-Royce (bottom).

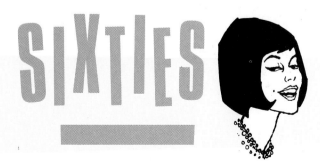

17

When they drew up the sheets, the bespectacled Beatle and his Japanese wife were also drawing up battle lines which should have been etched indelibly on the conscience of the world years before. Everybody knew the world was a mess, but only the kids were prepared to do something about it. And they were going to do it, whether it meant sticking flowers down the barrels of armed U.S. Marines, or rioting in the streets of Paris as the prelude to a General Strike which, in 1968, had the entire nation teetering on the brink of Civil War.

Six years previously, France had finally granted independence to Algeria, an unwilling concession to the wind of change which, in 1960, the English Prime Minister, Harold MacMillan, had warned was sweeping through the Dark Continent. The liberations offered by the European colonial powers during the 1950s were merely a prelude to the wave upon wave which followed over the next decade. In 1960 Belgium pulled out of the Congo, France from the Sahara and Cameroon, Italy from Somaliland, and Britain from Nigeria. Five years later, protracted negotiations between Rhodesia's Ian Smith and the British government ended when Rhodesia, too, declared Independence. And almost everywhere the withdrawal of the occupying powers saw the newly founded countries all but collapse beneath the weight of local and regional power struggles, a process which culminated in the horror of Biafra towards the end of the 1960s. A hopeless war with Nigeria, plague and disease, took the ultimate toll of this tiny secessionist borderland.

By the end of the decade, only South Africa, the richest of all African countries, remained wholly under white control, the apartheid or 'separate development' policies of the ruling Afrikaaner Nationalist Party ensuring not only the continuation of that particular practice, but also the nation's growing estrangement from the rest of the world, a process against which the ruling party were, and still are, cushioned by their country's immense mineral wealth.

Adam Faith

John Profumo

As early as 1963 the English pop singer, Adam Faith, was at the centre of a storm caused by his visit to the country. By the end of the decade, South Africa was unable to take part even in sporting events, such was the outrage at her treatment of her indigenous population. And while South Africa's withdrawal from the British Commonwealth in 1961, was seen by that country as a protest against British interference in domestic affairs, in Britain it was regarded with a feeling which approached relief, at least in as much as it saved Britain the embarrassment of having to continue to explain away the behaviour of the Afrikaaners. She had enough on her plate as it was.

The antics of the British secret services, which had at first horrified, then almost amused, the rest of the world during the 1950s, as the organisation lurched from one spy scandal to another, reached a climax of sorts in 1963, when it was revealed that the Secretary of State for War, John Profumo, had taken for his mistress a girl, Christine Keeler, who was also involved with a Soviet agent in London. Suggestions that the Russians were receiving secrets, through Keeler, from Profumo were taken with the utmost seriousness by Britain's western allies; coming after the defection of Kim Philby, and with the loss of so many NATO secrets to the Russians still fresh in many people's minds, the public revelations of what MacMillan described as "a silly scrape over a woman" snowballed into a political catastrophe which was to topple the Conservative government after more than 13 years in power.

Christine Keeler

For Harold MacMillan, the Profumo affair was the last straw. Britain's fourth post-war Prime Minister, he had been in power since 1957, but failing health had made recent years difficult to cope with. In 1962, he sacked seven Cabinet ministers in one go. Now, one year later, Harold Wilson the leader of the Opposition Labour Party was saying he had sacked the wrong ones. Before the year was out, MacMillan had resigned, stepping down in favour of Sir Alec Douglas-Home, who himself was to remain at Number 10 for less than a year.

Harold Wilson, the Yorkshire-born MP for Huyton, near Liverpool, came to power in October 1964, a success founded as much on the verbal gimmickry which characterised the Labour campaign as on any purely political considerations. 'Let's go with Labour!' shouted the button badges and sloganeers, while Wilson himself grabbed firmly the coat-tails of the burgeoning pop culture to talk of "A new Britain, a dynamic, expanding, confident . . . purposeful Britain, forged in the white heat of the technological revolution". He picked up on the promise, spouted everywhere from the popular broadsheets to the Sunday colour supplements, of a Britain on the move, a fashion world dominated by Carnaby Street, a music world dominated by The Beatles.

The Vote was still confined to the over-21s – when Screaming Lord Sutch campaigned in 1964, for that requirement to be reduced to 18 the outrage was as great as in 1983, when he demanded men wear their underpants outside their trousers. But Wilson knew that you didn't have to *be* young to think young. He allied himself to The Beatles, despite having no more of a connection with the Fab Four than an electoral accident which gave him a constituency in their own home town, his policies seemed guaranteed to give young people an easier ride than they had ever known before.

Swinging London, with its attendant visions of pop art and op art, became synonymous with the fresh new wind blowing through British politics; when The Beatles were awarded the MBE, at Wilson's instigation, for services to the British Empire, John Lennon summed up the establishment's bemusement when he admitted, "I thought you had to drive tanks and win wars to get the MBE". To everybody else, though, the honour was just one more nail in the coffin of the fusty, dusty, stale Britain which had drifted along in the years before Wilson's government ushered in this new age of enlightenment.

At the time of his election, Harold Wilson seemed to be offering the youth of his country an alternative. In the United States, that burden was carried, with even more dignity, by John F. Kennedy. The youngest President in American history, he represented the idealism of youth and for the majority of the American public, the White House and thus the U.S. as a whole, for his brief period in office, really did hold out the promise of a brave new world. Following as it did the blandness of the Eisenhower years, and the mass-paranoia of the McCarthy witch hunts, Kennedy's incumbency saw America finally awaken to her own potential. With his patronage of the space programme he presented America with a goal as far flung as his own hopes.

Further afield, his handling of the Cuban missile crisis established him as a world leader in every sense of the word. Whether in political or personal terms, his charisma was such that it reached out and touched people throughout the world. In telling people not to ask what their country could do for them, but what they could do for their country, he fostered an upsurge of faith and belief in his own country, at the same time engendering a new spirit of co-operation both at home and abroad. People responded to his rallying call both in word and deed – the Peace Corps, which he founded, took the power and affluence of the U.S. and attempted to channel it for the good of all mankind. His assassination, on November 22, 1963, was not to end the hopes and dreams of the people his rhetoric had inspired, but seriously altered the direction in which they could be channelled. Kennedy's successor, Lyndon B. Johnson, attempted to further his predecessor's vision on the domestic front, but this was not enough. The Vietnam war was gathering pace, and Johnson's inability to prevent that escalation saw the end of a dream. Suddenly the millions of people who had answered Kennedy's clarion call found themselves protesting against the selfsame establishment that they had once so wholeheartedly supported. But Johnson was not Kennedy, and the government became less and less responsive as the protests grew. What started as a youth protest swiftly gathered older and more influential supporters. And slowly a counter-culture began to form. Led by such eminent people as Dr. Timothy Leary, a distinguished professor from Harvard University, many people began to simply 'turn on and drop out' of society. Others, supported by names such as Martin Luther King and Joan Baez, preferred peaceful protest. Some, such as the Black Panthers and the Yippies, chose to answer violence with violence.

Harold Wilson celebrates Labour's 1964 election triumph.

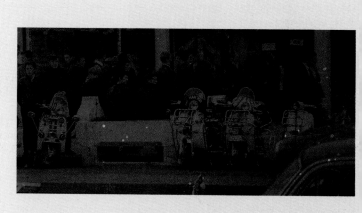

Everywhere you looked, the values of the old society were being challenged. Bank Holidays at Margate and Brighton were no longer the province of jovial holiday-makers in knotted hankies and rolled up trousers; bands of mods and rockers, besuited scooter-riding fops who lived for clothes, and died if they were caught in last night's sweater, on the one hand, and greasy leatherclad longhairs on powerful motorbikes on the other, tore apart the peaceful tranquility of the seaside towns with pitched battles on the beach and prom. Out in the North Sea, the BBC's monopoly of the nation's airwaves was finally ended by the birth, on March 28, 1964, of Radio Caroline. There was a time when pirates came armed to the teeth and plundered everything they could. Now they needed no more than a microphone, a transmitter and boxful of records, a leaking tub anchored safely in international waters and an audience who would faithfully tune into their wavelength every night for a diet of non-stop pop. At noon that Easter Saturday, anybody listening in to 197 metres MW was suddenly assailed with the sound of 'Can't Buy Me Love', The Beatles' latest chart topper. What else could they have played?

Mods at Margate.

On May 12, Radio Atlanta kicked into gear, on May 27, Radio Sutch beamed out from a disused war-time fort on Shivering Sands. Two days before Christmas, Radio London began regular transmissions; by the time the British Government finally moved in earnest against the pirates, with the August 1967 Marine Broadcasting Offences Act, one could scarcely twiddle the dial without running into one or other of the pirates. After they'd gone, of course, it was business as usual for the Beeb, and even the introduction of the new Radio One on September 30, with a staff comprised almost exclusively of former pirate DJs, couldn't stem the tide of black armbands and 'Wilson For Ex-Premier' badges which were worn with such pride by the pirates' former supporters.

Wilson's government retained power until the very end of the decade, but by 1967, the Summer Of Love, the euphoria which had accompanied the first half of his rule had finally faded, buried beneath a surfeit of good times, and followed so closely by a surfeit of anti-climaxes. In 1966, the England football team conquered the world to win the Jules Rimet Trophy, 4-2 against West Germany at Wembley. Less than 12 months later their crown was already slipping. They beat Austria in Vienna, and Spain at Wembley, but could only draw with Russia, while defeat at the hands of Scotland was rated as great a national tragedy as could be imagined. The Glasgow club, Celtic's, triumph in the European Cup that same year only rubbed salt into the wounds. Of course Scotland was part of the United Kingdom, but even at the best of times it was an uneasy alliance. The introduction of North Sea Gas, piped from Scottish waters, saw the call for Scottish nationalism grow loud; the government's decision to nationalise the shipyards which were at the heart of Scottish industry made it louder still.

As the horror of Vietnam was presented to the American people nightly during the evening news, even the more conservative, middle-aged began to question the sanity of a war that they seemed unable to win and worse, unable to end. The youngsters were no longer willing to emulate the example of the elders by merely petitioning and marching, the years had seen them become too cynical for that. Better to burn it all down and start again. Create a new world of love, brotherhood and peace. But how could this be accomplished in a land of civil strife and war? For many the answer was found in drugs. First marijuana, then LSD, then any other pill they could find. Then there were communes; people living and sharing together in their own self created world. Religion offered answers to others, and strange cults flowered. The Beatles' fascination with Eastern mysticism provoked tens of thousands of young Americans to look in this direction for answers.

The youth movement gathered momentum like a snowball. The protest marches grew bigger and bigger; the cries of dissent grew louder. The Doors' 'Unknown Soldier', Jefferson Airplane's 'Volunteers', Country Joe's 'Feel Like I'm Fixing To Die Rag', Arlo Guthrie's trip to 'Alice's Restaurant', put the most heartfelt rage of the youth movement to music as effectively as if their guitars had been machine guns and they had stood atop Capitol Hill and mowed down the Establishment in its own backyard. "Up against the wall, Motherfuckers", sang the Airplane in 'Volunteers', a rallying call which was responded to figuratively, if not literally, by everyone who heard it. And as their anger became greater, the Establishment's responses grew heavier handed.

THE 60s

The Beatles contemplate the wisdom of the Maharishi.

Jim Morrison

Mao Tse Tung

By the time of Robert Kennedy's assassination in 1968, the last hope of his brother's idealism was lost forever. Richard Nixon was the logical successor for this disenchanted nation. But surprisingly, the disillusionment was reserved strictly for the government and politics in general. A new wind was blowing through America, and a new society was being created. Black civil rights were becoming a reality. Women's liberation was occurring in every suburban home across the land. Other minorities were benefiting in the wake of this liberal explosion. If the government wasn't responding the way the people wanted, then in an echo of Kennedy's famous words the people were making it happen themselves. On the domestic front at least, the American dream was being realised for the first time by all.

Tricky Dicky on the election trail.

The antithesis to America's expanding consciousness was taking place almost simultaneously on the other side of the world, in China. In October 1964, coincidentally within the same few days as Harold Wilson's election and Nikita Kruschev's deposition, the People's Republic exploded their first atomic bomb, becoming in the process the fifth nuclear power. China's relations with the Soviet Union, with whom she shared the largest portion of her borders, began a slow process of disintegration in 1960 when Mao Tse Tung highlighted the ideological differences between the two Communist nations when he described the Soviet leaders as 'revisionists'. Armed skirmishes along the disputed Sino-Soviet border heightened the tension, particularly during the latter half of the decade when the so-called Cultural Revolution saw western access to, and influence over, China come to a standstill as Mao attempted to secure his nation's social boundaries even as he was fighting to maintain her political limits.

The Middle East, too, posed a serious threat to world security. Whereas America's involvement in Vietnam, and the joint Russo-Chinese attempts to aid the Communist Hanoi government, did much to defuse the situation between the two eastern powers, the constant state of armed peace which surrounded Israel and her Arab neighbours continually threatened to explode. In 1967, it did so, although the speed with which tiny Israel was to crush the combined forces of Egypt, Syria and Jordan was to induce at least a temporary impasse; the vast territorial gains which Israel made during the Six Days War included the fertile west bank of the River Jordan and, of equal political import, saw the reuniting of the City of Jerusalem, which had previously been divided along similar lines to Berlin.

Analogous with the Sixties, perhaps even indicative of them, were The Beatles. Like the decade itself, they burst onto the scene, a fresh, almost naive unit whose promises were simply taken too seriously. Never before had a mere Pop group represented so much, to so many, as did The Beatles; neither would their impact ever be repeated. But with the glories that their almost immediate success brought, came a slow, painful disintegration. The Beatles had touched the world, now the world was touching them, a large, stumpy finger thrust into the epicentre of the storm and turning everything upside down.

The Beatles in 1963, the year Beatlemania swept the country.

The Beatles 'Sergeant Pepper' album released in June 1967, was simply another long-playing record for them, albeit one which had been created away from the pressures attendant upon them before they made the decision to stop touring. For the world at large, however, it was an artistic statement of the highest degree, and one which quite literally changed the course of popular music. Certainly its success was such that The Beatles themselves could never hope to recover, at least from within the strait-jacket of their own public image. Thus, they began to diversify; John turned to experimentation and art, Paul towards sentimentality, George towards mysticism, Ringo towards pool tables and Butlins. The death of their mentor, Brian Epstein, whilst The Beatles were 'holidaying' in North Wales with the Maharishi, carved another line of their own epitaph. Like Icarus of the legend, The Beatles had flown too near to the sun; now they were falling back to earth. Previously they had seemed untouchable; now they were fair game for anybody.

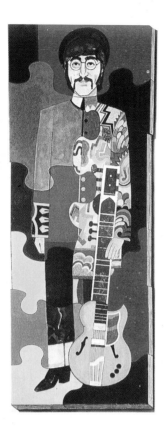

The Beatles in their psychedelic period.

The British police, still triumphant from their arrest, on drugs charges, of The Rolling Stones', Mick Jagger, Keith Richard and Brian Jones, now turned their attention to The Beatles. Two years previously, such audacity would have been unthinkable. The band's personal behaviour, previously regarded with the patient humour of an indulgent parent watching an exuberant child at play, suddenly seemed something more sinister than simple boyish high spirits. When a Los Angeles drifter, Charles Manson, incited his 'family' of runaways, drop-outs and drug fiends to massacre actress Sharon Tate and friends at her home in Cielo Drive, Manson's own personal fascination with The Beatles, the belief that they were sending him messages through the medium of their music, was given exposure almost as great as the crimes themselves. The Beatles, like the decade which they epitomised, had suddenly become something unholy. But while their own decline was to meet no more than the token resistance of one-quarter of their line-up, Paul McCartney's belief that if they could only get back to playing rock 'n' roll they would be worth saving, the general idealism which they themselves had done so much to foster was still to have one last great fling.

Woodstock was the culmination of three years of pop festivals, a three-day celebration of the New Society, staged in a muddy field on a farm in the Catskill Mountains in upstate New York. The cream of pop culture was there, and for everybody who bemoaned the absence of the founding fathers of the scene, The Beatles, The Rolling Stones and Bob Dylan, there were several thousand more who were more than satisfied with the eventual bill of fare; The Who, once big daddies of the Swinging London Carnaby Street scene, now breaking new ground as the purveyors of the first rock opera; Jimi Hendrix, a vision of black America dominating a white man's world; The Jefferson Airplane and The Grateful Dead, spokesmen of the hippy society whose dream Woodstock quite literally fulfilled; Country Joe McDonald, whose "One, two three, what are we fighting for?" refrain had been taken up as the anthem of everybody warring against the war, and Crosby, Stills, Nash & Young, the first soft rock supergroup whose sound was to so dominate America in the early 1970s.

★ ★ ★ ★ ★ ☆

Canadian songstress Joni Mitchell wrote a song about the festival without even being there, an epic film of the event broke box office records throughout the western world, 10 sides of vinyl preserved the music of that rainy weekend for all posterity, and the memory of half a million kids camped out in their canvas city simply grooving to the music is impressed on the mind of everybody who ever heard of the affair. There were three deaths – one O.D., one burst appendix and one run over by a tractor – and two births, few fights and considerably less arrests than might have been made in a concrete city of a similar size over a similar timespan. But for all its success, for all the peace and love, for all the myriad other positive points in its favour, Woodstock stood not a chance of becoming the new dawn which its organisers so idealistically portrayed it as. Max Yasgur's ploughed field was no Garden of Eden, and while the evils of society might have been held at bay for 72 blissful hours in the middle of August, on Monday it was back to work and before long, even the memory of the festival was no more tangible than the smell of damp which still clung to your sleeping bag. Rather, Woodstock was one final gesture of defiance as the dream came to an end, a long-haired Nero fiddling while the incense burner set the city alight. By the time The Rolling Stones set about building a Woodstock of their own, at Altamont Speedway at the beginning of December, only a last, hardy, few even thought about rekindling that original spark. They came now for the music, pure and simple; there was no altruism at Altamont, just 400,000 kids trying not to get their heads busted by the cue-wielding Angels employed by the Stones for security purposes. Twenty-five days later, the Sixties came to an end.

Like the people who built them, the Sixties will never be repeated. On July 20, 1969, man walked on the moon; almost 20 years later he is as far from the rest of the planets as he ever was. The New Britain which Harold Wilson promised would be forged "in the white heat of technology" is still waiting its turn on the blacksmith's anvil, and the lessons learned so painfully in the jungles of Vietnam seem to have been absorbed only by the film world. The predictions of a brave new tomorrow which once assailed us from every angle have yet to be fulfilled. Only now, nobody expects them to be.

The beliefs of the Sixties, we are told today, were gullible, naive, doomed to failure. And maybe they were. But they were beliefs all the same, concrete beliefs which sustained a generation through a decade during which progress and turbulence walked hand in hand. Perhaps the decade wasn't as innocent as it was painted – looking back on the catalogue of iniquities which dominated the news, it seems hard to believe people ever thought it was. But even as the passing years catapult the Sixties' kids ever closer towards those watershed years which, in their guileless youth, seemed a lifetime away, that innocence is perhaps the most palpable of all the emotions unleashed by those 10 crazy years almost a quarter of a century ago.

It is with us everywhere, from the flickering reruns of old TV sitcoms to the two bob bits which still turn up in our small change, from the chance find of a dated photograph – Aunt Jean on the Kings Road, 1967 – to the dog-eared copy of Tolkien, up there on the shelf with The Bible. But most importantly, it is still with us in the music, and that is something neither time nor talk will ever take away.

SIXTIES

AMEN CORNER: '(IF PARADISE IS) HALF AS NICE' was this Welsh septet's fifth hit single, reaching number one in January, 1969. The band hailed from Cardiff, first hitting the chart during the summer of 1967 with the moody 'Gin House Blues'. This was followed by the less successful 'World Of Broken Hearts', before the band hit their stride in the new year when first, 'Bend Me Shape Me', then 'High In The Sky' gave them two of the year's most memorable Top Ten smashes. Sadly, they were to manage but one further hit 'Hello Suzie', after 'Half As Nice' took them to the top. When their record company folded late in the year, Amen Corner swiftly followed suit. While the brass section, Allan Jones and Mike Smith, formed Judas Jump with two one-time members of The Herd, the remainder of the group – vocalist Andy Fairweather-Low, Neil Jones (guitar), Clive Taylor (bass), Dennis Byron (drums) and Blue Weaver (organ) – remained together as Fairweather, and enjoyed one more hit, 'Natural Sinner', in 1970. Since then, Blue Weaver has worked primarily as a session musician, while Fairweather-Low, the band's principal songwriter, launched a rewarding, if sporadic, solo career, the highlight of which was his 1975 composition 'Wide Eyed And Legless'.

Amen Corner, with singer Andy Fairweather-Low (foreground).

THE ARCHIES: 'SUGAR SUGAR' was originally written for The Monkees; when they turned it down, their music director, Don Kirshner, gave it instead to The Archies, who immediately premièred it on their Saturday morning TV show, a weekly event in which Archie loved Betty, Reggie loved Veronica and the drummer loved the old jalopy which would get him from Riverdale High to Pop's Choklit Shoppe. There was no sex, no violence, no drugs . . . there was no group. The Archies were a cartoon, but that didn't stop 'Sugar Sugar' taking them to number one on both sides of the Atlantic, for four weeks in the U.S. the very same week as the Woodstock Festival took place: surely one of the decade's greatest ironies. 'Sugar Sugar' began an eight-week U.K. chart-topping run in October 1969.

Chris Farlowe

CHRIS FARLOWE: 'OUT OF TIME' was written by Mick Jagger and Keith Richard, one of several Stones songs which Chris Farlowe (real name John Deighton) covered during his own Sixties' career. Two others, 'Think' and 'Ride On Baby', were minor hits for Farlowe on either side of 'Out Of Time', but it is for 'Out Of Time' that he is best remembered today. Number one for one week in July 1966, the song established Farlowe and his band, The Thunderbirds, as one of the country's biggest concert draws, although he was never able to repeat his original success. He finally retired from the music business in 1972, surfacing only briefly in 1975 to promote a reissue of his greatest hit, and it was left to his former lieutenants to enjoy the greatest fame; crack country-style guitarist Albert Lee later formed Heads, Hands And Feet (a band which numbered Chas Hodges, of Chas & Dave, amongst its members) before making a very profitable move out to California, keyboard wizard Dave Greenslade put together Colosseum and Greenslade, both of whom met with some success during the early-mid Seventies, while drummer Carl Palmer become one third of Emerson, Lake & Palmer after further stints with Arthur Brown's Crazy World and Atomic Rooster.

The Kinks

Amen Corner

The Moody Blues

Chris Farlowe

The Honeycombs

THE FOUNDATIONS: 'BABY, NOW THAT I'VE FOUND YOU' was this multi-national septet's first, and greatest hit, reaching number one in September 1967. Lining up as Alan Warner (guitar, vocals), Colin Young (guitar), Tony Gomesz (organ), Pat Bourke (sax), Eric Allendale (trombone), Peter MacBeth (bass) and Tim Harris (drums), the band boasted passports originating from London, Barbados, Jamaica, Ceylon and Dominica; an ethnic combination which was not, however, reflected in their music. Bright and breezy, The Foundations epitomised British Pop in the months following 'Sergeant Pepper', and over the next two years were to score two further Top 10 hits ('Build Me Up Buttercup' and 'In The Bad, Bad Old Days'), together with three lesser successes.

THE HONEYCOMBS: 'HAVE I THE RIGHT?' was the first of four hits for this North London outfit, an instant number one in July 1964 which, coupled with the success of fellow Londoners The Dave Clark 5, prompted a rash of news stories predicting the downfall of The Beatles and the rise of a new North London beat sound. Of course it was not to be, The Honeycombs digging their own grave by disappearing on a lengthy tour of Australia at the very same time as they should have been consolidating the success of their first single either at home or in America. By the time they returned, all most people could remember of the group was that they had a female drummer, Honey Lantree. The rest of the group — Dennis D'Ell (vocals), Martin Murray (guitar), Alan Ward (guitar), John Lantree (bass), might not even have existed! In the event, the group were to muster three further hit singles, but only the last, 'That's The Way' came close to recapturing their debut glory, reaching number 12 in August 1965.

THE KINKS: 'YOU REALLY GOT ME' reached number one in August, 1964, the first hit (but third single) for another North London outfit. Led by the Davies brothers, Ray (vocals) and Dave (guitar), the band's earliest line-up was completed by Mick Avory (drums) and Pete Quaife (bass). The elder Davies, Ray, wrote the majority of the band's material, and throughout the Sixties his pen ensured that The Kinks were second only to The Beatles and The Stones in terms of musical creativity; indeed, The Kinks were very often some way ahead of their more illustrious contemporaries, losing out in the final analysis more because they lagged behind in the personality stakes than anything else (anyone could tell you the names of the individual Beatles and Stones, but who could do the same with The Kinks?). Nevertheless, by the end of the decade The Kinks had scored an astonishing 14 Top 20 hits, including three number ones – 'Tired Of Waiting For You' and 'Sunny Afternoon' complete the trilogy. Since then, the band has soldiered on (with a changing personnel behind the Davies brothers) with a resolute spirit which, again, has left many of their contemporaries at the starting post and which, in worldwide terms, has ensured that today, The Kinks are at least as popular as they ever were during their so-called heyday in the Sixties.

PROCOL HARUM: 'A WHITER SHADE OF PALE' was a stunning combination of classical melody and surrealist lyrics which took Procol Harum to number one in May 1967 and which, by the end of the year, had outsold anything even The Beatles or the Stones were to release during that magical 12 months. That the band were never able to follow-up their success was largely immaterial. Over the next decade they were to release a succession of albums which were, for the most part, at least as inventive as that first hit, but which remained considerably closer in execution to the band's own abilities than did 'Shade . . . ' Shortly after the single's release it was revealed that the band's then-current line-up of Gary Brooker (vocals, piano), Matthew Fisher (organ), Ray Royer (guitar), Bobby Harrison (drums) and Dave Knights (bass) had not all been present at the recording session, and that other musicians appeared on the record. Following this Royer and Harrison were sacked in favour of drummer Barrie Wilson and latter-day guitar maestro and Hendrix worshipper, Robin Trower, and in this form Procol Harum launched into their period of greatest musical accomplishment with such albums as 'Shine On Brightly', 'A Salty Dog' and 'Home'. They also maintained a steady, if somewhat sporadic stream of hit singles, although only 'Hamburg', in October 1967, came anywhere near to eclipsing the phenomenal success of that very first record.

Procol Harum

THE MOODY BLUES: 'GO NOW' was the second single by this Birmingham outfit, a majestic song with a memorable descending riff which deservedly hit the top spot in January 1965. Lining up as Denny Laine (guitar, vocals), Mike Pinder (keyboards), Ray Thomas (vocals, horns), Graeme Edge (drums) and Clint Warwick (bass), the band followed this success with a smash hit American tour, opening for The Beatles, and for a short time even shared the Fab Four's manager, Brian Epstein. However, further chart glory eluded them – 'From The Bottom Of My Heart', in June 1965, came closest to emulating 'Go Now' when it reached number 22 – and finally Laine and Warwick quit, to be replaced by John Lodge and Justin Hayward. Their arrival signalled a complete change in direction for the Moodys, and in autumn, 1967, the band stunned the world with the epochal 'Days Of Future Years Passed' album, a set which in many ways surpassed even 'Sergeant Pepper' in terms of conception and delivery. Simultaneously, the single 'Nights In White Satin' returned the band to the Top 20, and subsequent Moody's albums, whilst occasionally suffering from a misplaced desire to recreate the ingenuity of 'Days...' ensured the band's admission to the highest echelons of Pop iconography. Original singer Denny Laine enjoyed sporadic solo success before joining Paul McCarney's Wings in the seventies. He was last heard of in the bankruptcy court.

THE TREMELOES: 'SILENCE IS GOLDEN' was released in April 1967, the second hit – and first number one – for a band who were to all but dominate the British pop scene as the Sixties wound to a close. Originally formed in 1959 as the backing group for singer Brian Poole, the combination had a run of eight hits between 1963 ('Twist And Shout') and 1965, when Poole left to go solo. Lining up as Alan Blakeley (guitar, vocals), Dave Munden (drums), Chip Hawkes (bass) and Ricky West (guitar) the band suffered two flop singles before 'Here Comes My Baby' took them to number four in February 1967. 'Silence Is Golden' followed, and in August, 'Even The Bad Times Are Good' returned the group to the top five. Thereafter, The Tremeloes enjoyed a solid run of success for the next four years, losing momentum only after they went public with the belief that their past hits had all been 'rubbish' and that the people who bought them were 'morons'. The hits dried up, and by the time the band were ready to repent – and reinstated all the old 'rubbish' in their live set, they were already forgotten!

THE SEARCHERS: 'NEEDLES AND PINS' gave this Liverpudlian band the second of the three number one singles they were to enjoy between June 1963 and April 1964 ('Sweets For My Sweet' and 'Don't Throw Your Love Away' were the others). Formed in 1960 by Mike Pender (guitar), Tony Jackson (bass), Chris Curtis (drums) and John McNally (guitar), The Searchers, for a short time all but dominated the Merseybeat scene, lying second only to The Beatles both in terms of popularity and success. Out of 14 hit singles, enjoyed over a two and a half year period between 1963 and 1966, only four failed to crack the Top 20, while 'Sugar And Spice' was deprived of the top spot only by fellow Liverpudlians Gerry & The Pacemakers. Neither were the band to fold once the hits stopped coming: instead they moved into the cabaret circuit, resurfacing periodically with new releases which somehow managed to sound just as sweet as any of the band's better-known Sixties' classics.

THE 60s